A MAGIC CIRCLE BOOK

THE LONG LINE OF LETTERS

written by **GLADYS BARTHOLOMEW**

illustrated by **Joan Paley**

THEODORE CLYMER
SENIOR AUTHOR, READING 360

GINN AND COMPANY
A XEROX COMPANY

1

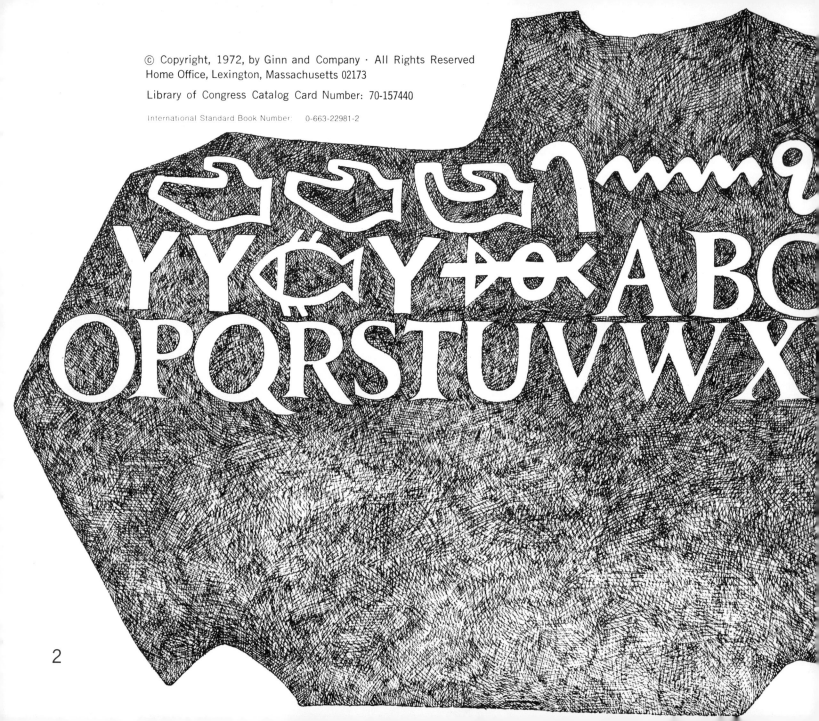

2

THE LONG LINE
OF LETTERS

3

Thousands of years ago men had no alphabet. When they wanted to keep a record of what they had seen or done, they drew a picture story. Can you read this picture story?

For a long time men used picture stories. Then as they had more ideas and wanted to share these ideas, they needed a better way to write them. They began to use marks like these Y, ⅂, ◁ instead of pictures to stand for words.

Later a mark was used to stand for each sound in a word. The marks which stood for the sounds have been changed many times, and they have become the alphabet we use today.

It took more than a thousand years for all these changes to take place. Since no person is one thousand years old, no one can tell us exactly how the alphabet came to be. But many people have studied the pictures and marks left on rocks and cliff walls. These people have given us some ideas about the beginning of our alphabet.

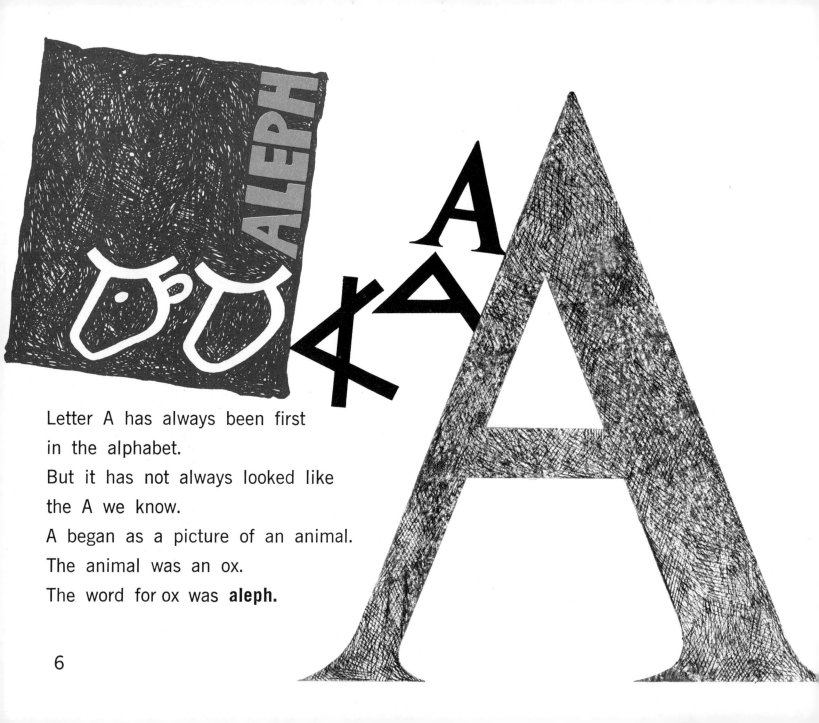

Letter A has always been first
in the alphabet.
But it has not always looked like
the A we know.
A began as a picture of an animal.
The animal was an ox.
The word for ox was **aleph.**

6

Letter B
may have first been
the picture of a house.
Beth was the word
which meant house.

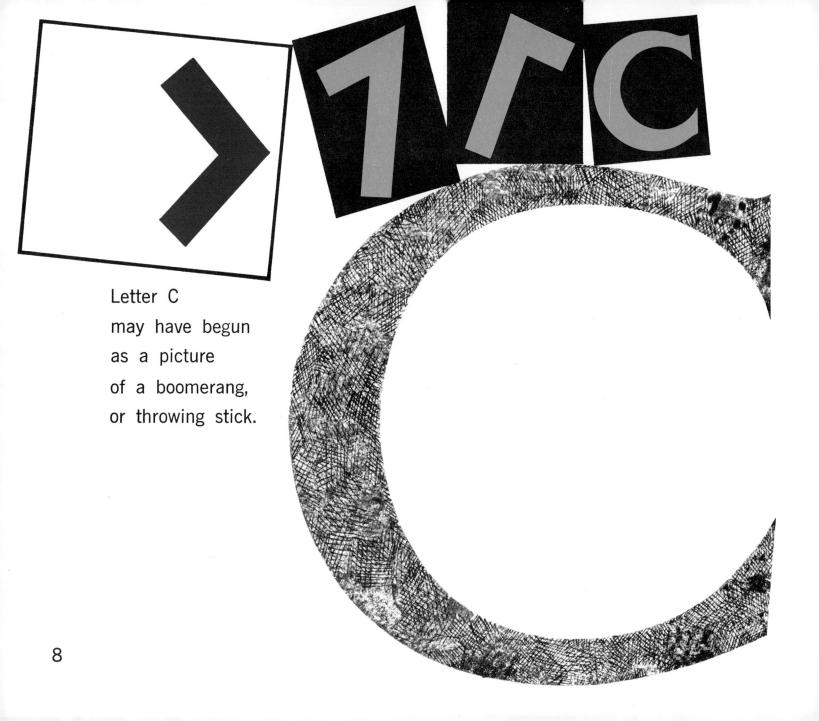

Letter C
may have begun
as a picture
of a boomerang,
or throwing stick.

8

An early letter D
was the picture of a door.

Letter E may have begun
as a picture of a man
holding his hands up.
The picture
may have meant
thank you or joy.

10

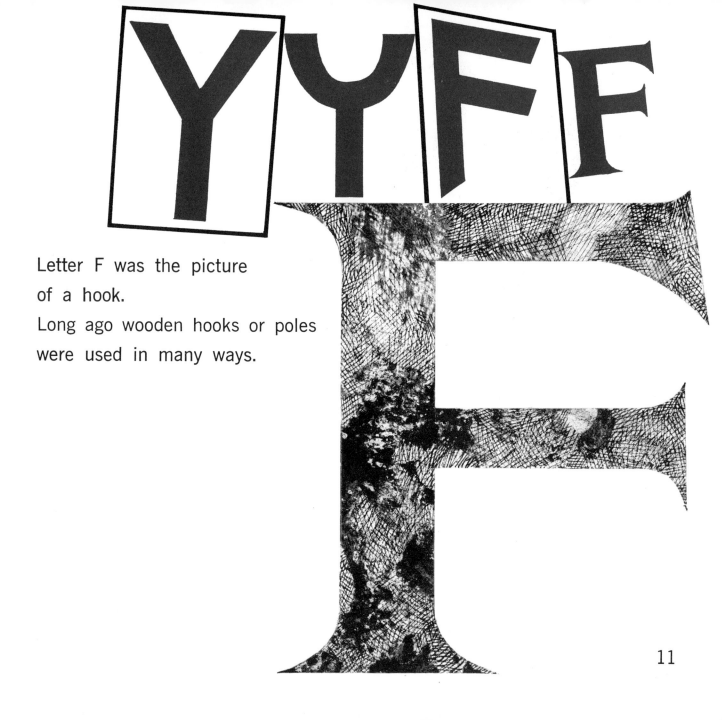

Letter F was the picture
of a hook.
Long ago wooden hooks or poles
were used in many ways.

11

Remember that letter C began
as a picture of a boomerang.
Letter G began the same way.
G became a different letter
when a tail was added to C.

12

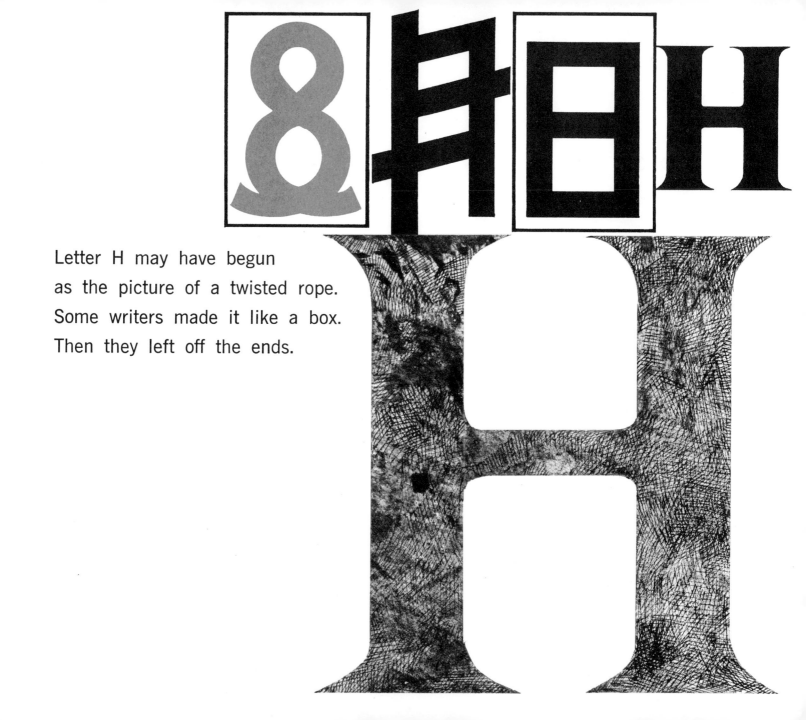

Letter H may have begun
as the picture of a twisted rope.
Some writers made it like a box.
Then they left off the ends.

The picture of a hand
was the beginning of letter I.
Later it was a straight line.

Letter J is a new letter
in the long line of letters.
It was first used
when a tail was added
to letter I.

15

Letter K, like letter I,
began as a picture
of a hand.
But this picture showed
the inside of the hand.

Letter L may have begun
as a picture of a crooked staff,
which men used to herd sheep.
Some writers turned it around.

A picture of waves on the sea may have been the beginning of letter M.

Long ago the word for snake was **nahas.**
Many people believe that letter N
began as a picture of a snake.
Later the picture stood for a fish.
The word for fish was **nun.**

The picture of an eye
may have been
an early letter O.
Later the long lines
were left off.

20

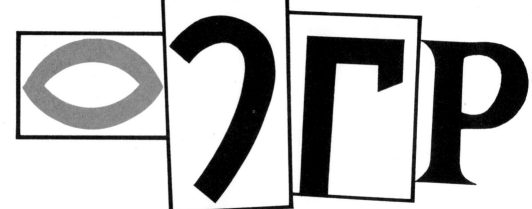

Letter P may have begun
as the picture of a mouth.
Then writers made a hook shape.
Later writers turned it around.

No one is sure
how letter Q began.
It may have been a picture
of a monkey.
Today when we write Q
in a word,
we usually write U
after it.

Do you think letter R
looks like a man's head?
R was first drawn as a picture
of a head.
The name for head was **resh.**

Letter S may have begun
as a picture of a tooth.
The word for tooth was **shin.**

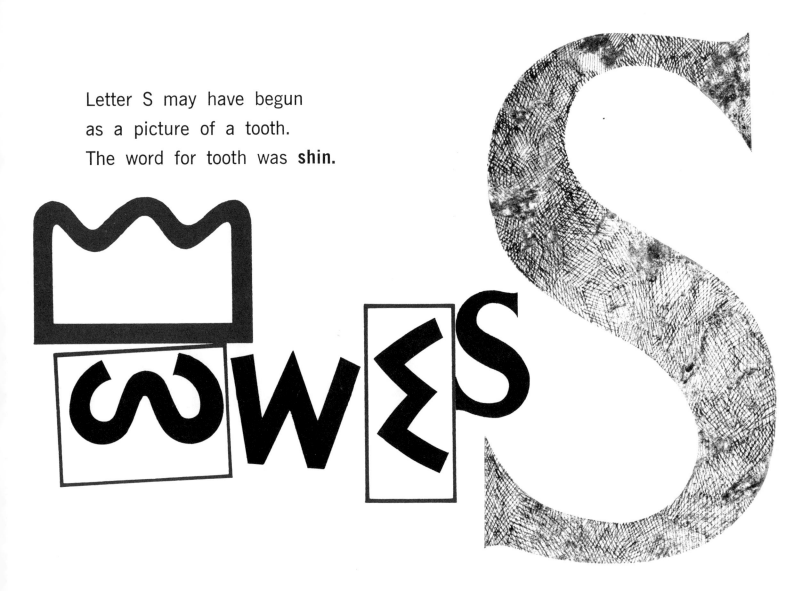

The first letter T was made
like a large X and meant
brand, or mark.
By turning the X,
writers made a cross.
Then writers
left the top off the cross
and made the T as we do today.

25

Letters U, V, and W
began alike.
For a long time,
V stood for the sounds
that U, V, and W
stand for today.
Then writers rounded
letter V when they wanted
a vowel sound.
The rounded letter
became letter U.
Later writers
put two V's together.
V V became letter W.
However,
it was called "double U"
instead of "double V."

u u U V
w w U V
W W

27

Letter X
may have begun
as the picture
of a fish.

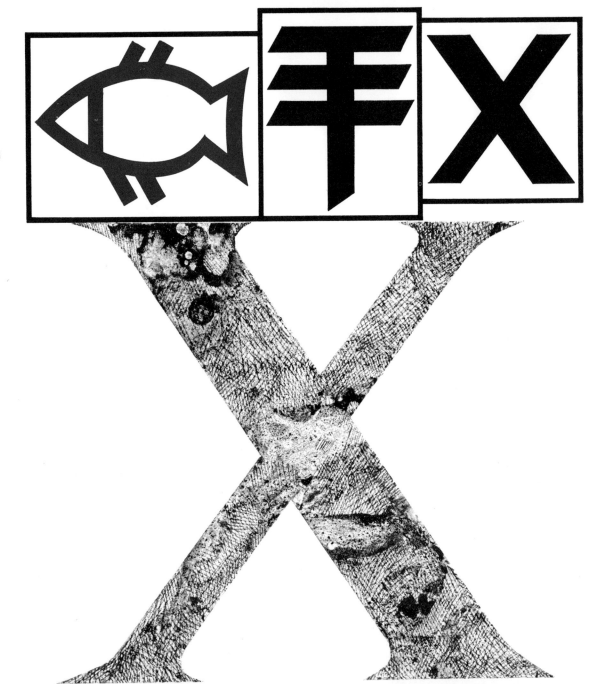

Letter Y,
like letters F, U, V, and W,
began as the picture of a hook.
Today letter Y may be
a consonant letter
or a vowel letter.

At the end of
the long line of letters
comes letter Z.
At one time,
it may have looked
like two sticks.
Two sticks stood
for the word **zayin**
which meant weapon.

30

Now you have seen the long line of
letters — our alphabet. Do you think it would
be easy to read or write a story without the
alphabet? Try it. Write a story using only
pictures and have someone try to read it.

ABCDEFGHIJK 7654321
PRINTED IN THE UNITED STATES OF AMERICA